Creating a Culture of Welcome

in the Local Church

Alison Gilchrist

Assistant Curate, St Cuthbert's, Fulwood, Preston

GROVE BOOKS LIMITED
RIDLEY HALL RD CAMBRIDGE CB3 9HU

Contents

Acknowledgment

I would like to thank the members of the Grove Evangelism group for their support and help in the editing stage. Thanks are due of course to Alan for the excellent Bible study material that is included on the supporting web page at www.grovebooks.co.uk—thanks, you are a diamond geezer! Further thanks are also owed to the worshipping community of St Thomas' Church, Blackpool who, after shaky first impressions, journeyed with me as together we learned how to grow towards a 'truer love.' And finally to Robert, Keira and Raegen without whose unfailing love and support nothing of these past 14 years would have been possible.

The Cover Illustration is by Peter Ashton

First Impression May 2004
ISSN 1367-0840
ISBN 1 85174 562 9

Initial Impressions— A Common Experience?

1

Recently I had to attend the out-patients department of the local hospital with my eldest daughter.

Hospitals are not known to be places we are keen to visit or which provide especially warm receptions, but the details of the appointment arrived along with a pamphlet aimed at putting us as ease, 'welcoming' us if you will. The demeanour of the staff on the department lived up to the brochure's preparation, as they received us with smiles and warm-hearted courtesy. This reactivated deliberations on how the church tackles the matter of welcome, because for many I have met during my ministry—as a staff member in a parish and since—the prospect of attending a service is as alarming, if not more so, than a visit to the hospital.

My first Sundays at church as an adult, were, if I am honest, painful. Though I had had some positive contact with the church through a 'Mother and Toddler' group it facilitated, I still felt trepidation as I towed my two young children down the church path that first Sunday morning. Fred, bright of face and firm of handshake, alleviated my apprehension, reminding me of my beloved grandfather who had done the same job in the church where I was taken as a child. But most people do not have that history and the church is an unknown place.

For many the prospect of attending a service is as alarming, if not more so, than a visit to the hospital

Keeping two lively toddlers in check for almost an hour-and-a-half (whilst trying to deal with the various books and sheets of paper needed to follow what was going on) began to wear me down and I was glad to hear that we were about to sing our final hymn. Gathering up the books, paper and children I headed for the door only to find my exit blocked by a throng of chatty folk clutching cups and consuming biscuits. Would I like to stay and join them? asked the kindly cleric at the door, as I shook his hand. Not on your nelly I thought, whilst smiling and proffering the excuse that my husband needed dinner, though I might stay on another occasion.

Having steeled myself for a further visit I hoped that familiarity would alleviate the logistical problems if nothing else. Regrettably things proceeded in a like manner until the reprieve of the last song came and once more I headed for the door. Surely this week I could manage a few minutes for a coffee, and perhaps the children would like juice and a biscuit? Could I brush the vicar off again or was I trapped? Not wishing to appear too rude, I decided to stay. Having found the dispensing point, once more I had to prove myself an adept performer, juggling juice, biscuits and coffee to a safe place, where after unburdening myself of the food and drink, I clutched the children close, not wanting to be left alone in a writhing mass of bantering congregants who seemed to be best of friends and not in the least interested in sharing their enthusiasms with me.

I am now an ordinand nearing the end of my training and despite being on the 'inside,' I still face similar situations when attending a church new to me. Books and sheets abound. I am almost always thrust to the front of the church, the only area with space, leaving me unsure when to sit or stand. Without some direction I still do not get to the page in time to join in, and looking over to see if I can spy where we are from someone else's book frequently results in hostile glares.

My children have reached their teens, so sadly they are old enough to sense the lack of welcome proffered, and now vote with their feet. This particular point screams at me, not just because of the situation facing my own children, but because I have read the statistics and know that Peter Brierley was correct when he informed us that the 'tide was running out.'[1]

'Fellowship time' after the service is often an exclusive club where the outsider never catches sight of a friendly face approaching to say hello. So after a solitary shuffle in the corner until they lose heart, they make a bid for the door never to be seen again. What I have shared with numerous people, many of whom will probably never 'darken our doors' again, has mirrored my own experience, with some being more painful:

- leaving in tears having had no idea how to follow the words of the liturgy because no one gave out details of which book or page numbers;
- having someone turn away quite deliberately rather than sharing the peace;
- receiving a 'telling off' because a lively toddler chatted during the service;
- being told to 'Move! That's my seat!'

All this seems very different to the New Millennium Challenge to the Churches.[2]

- We will make you welcome.
- We will be family friendly.
- We will make sure you can hear clearly.
- We will be practical and relevant.
- We will help you explore answers to your deepest questions.
- We will offer you time to stop and think in a busy life.
- We will help you make sense of the Bible and who Jesus is.
- We will make sure your visit will be helpful and challenging.
- We will help you discover for yourself God's love, acceptance and forgiveness.
- We will offer you the chance to make a new start.

How Others Have Seen It

In her book *Be My Guest* Vivian Hall includes the experience of one man, who set about completing his own survey of the treatment 'guests' receive on attending church:

> Over the years I have sung and lectured in just about every type of church you can name. This exposure has given me a fairly good education as to what kind of people attend church. But why they attend still puzzles me.
>
> To date, of the 195 churches I have visited, I was spoken to only once by someone other than the official 'greeter'—and that was to ask me to please move my feet.[3]

Hall goes on to say 'Ouch! What an indictment on churches. Could this man have been in your church or mine?' An American who provides training for churches seeking to be more welcoming recounts his experience on arriving to run such an event:

> When I drove up to the church there was not a single sign that made me feel welcome. Only signs that said, 'Church parking only, all violators will be towed at the owner's expense.' I was confronted by a set of heavy solid wood doors, which were closed and nobody was in sight to welcome me. Just a sign that said, 'Doors locked during weekdays. Use office doors Monday through Friday from 9 amto 5 pm.'

After I entered the building I saw several people who were speaking to each other and nobody was nearby to welcome me. Not a single person said hello or even gave me eye contact. Just an usher who was positioned at the entrance of the sanctuary who handed me a bulletin without uttering a word.

I found my way to a pew and sat alone. As people began to fill most of the pews, not a single person sat anywhere nearby or even acknowledged me.

As the service began, the pastor gave a general greeting to anyone who was new and asked those in attendance to fill out the 'act of friendship' pad at the end of each aisle. Since I was sitting at the opposite end of the pew and nobody was anywhere near the end where the tablets were placed, the 'act of friendship' pad was never passed to me.

At the end of worship visitors were asked to join the congregation in the parlour for coffee and fellowship. I followed the crowd to the parlour and helped myself to a cup of coffee. There I stood alone, sipping on my cup. Nobody ever noticed me until I was introduced as the guest speaker. When a woman remarked that this was the friendliest church she had ever attended it was a contrast to what I had experienced. However, which experience was correct? Both were. For this woman, who has so many friends in the church, the church is indeed a friendly church. But for myself, the stranger in their midst, it was anything but a friendly church.[4]

This, the experience of far too many, highlights some of the very simple things we do not take into account. Expending energy on evangelistic programmes and encouraging members to invite folk may not bear fruit if this is the nature of first impressions they are faced with. As in all things there are exceptions. Some churches do warmly welcome new folk and integrate them into the life of the worshipping community. Churches with an *ethos of welcome* are fewer than I would hope.

A Little Research

As an outreach worker for an inner city parish that has seen growth by the hundreds over the past decade but where my job description still required giving a quarter of my time to 'welcome,' I endeavoured to find out why people did not come back. Of those I managed to follow up, most said they felt discomfited by the unfamiliar situation, self conscious, particularly during the singing and other parts that involved their response, and that no-one but the staff had spoken to them. When pressed most said if they had made a personal contact who had invited them to return, they most probably would have, although I note here a worrying point that continually challenged my practice. If someone did come back a second week, though church members had been introduced on the first, chatted merrily and encouraged them to come again, they did not keep a watchful eye out or excuse themselves from their 'buddies' to speak. One valuable suggestion I have heard comes from Nigel McCulloch, now the Bishop of Manchester, whose advice to regular churchgoers was to spend the first three minutes after a service seeking out and speaking to someone new, before heading towards friends.

The following is indicative:

In a study of churches across North America, 85% of the church members surveyed agreed with this statement: 'In our congregation, people go out of their way to be friendly to strangers and newcomers.' In growing churches, however, 98% agreed with that statement. In rapidly declining churches, the level of agreement with this statement was sometimes below 50%. Think what it would be like to visit a church in which half of those present were not willing to take the initiative to talk with you![5]

For the fullest research account of the UK church see *Gone But Not Forgotten* by Richter and Francis, who look at changing patterns, attitudes, culture, and the cost of commitment.[6]

2

A Theology Of Welcome— Building A Framework

The Business World

Welcoming people—being hospitable—is big business these days. Typing the word 'welcome' into a search engine in your PC will throw up thousands of sites dedicated to just this issue. Their attention-grabbing home pages always include 'Welcome to…' from recruitment agencies specializing in staff trained in the field, to universities offering courses in hospitality management and including the site of an American firm running a chain of steakhouses called 'Rare Hospitality'—which did strike me as a good title for this booklet! But the whole matter of welcome and hospitality is taken very seriously by those who are keen to have us visit, shop/eat at, or join their organization—objectives not dissimilar to our own.

Welcoming people—being hospitable—is big business these days

McDonald's is one such company whose entire ethos is geared around making us feel welcome and ensuring that we 'call again.' Its prescriptive 750-page training manual, for those who take the 'McJob,' includes a section on how employees are to greet customers, directing them to make eye contact and to smile. ASDA (Wal-Mart) have of late installed greeters at the entrance to their stores. Paul Nixon has picked up their philosophy and writes:

> We live in a customer service era. Churches, for the most part, are not in the lead here. Rather, we find secular organizations and companies like Disney and Wal-Mart are the ones raising the bar for how people expect to be treated. The institutions that will thrive and grow in this new century will increasingly be measured against such rising standards of excellence.[7]

If these analogies are too commercial for you, might I offer the English Tourist Board. In keeping with its very nature and name, it is usually known for being somewhat genteel and fairly reserved, giving accolades to well run country houses and quaint tea shops. It is not an institution normally known for its vigorous marketing strategies. But I find that they too are taking welcome exceedingly seriously, and they offer a training package, at the end of which participants receive a certificate to display in their own establishments, declaring each person to be a qualified 'Welcome Host committed to the objectives of the Welcome Host Scheme.'

Followers of the One who 'came not to be served but to serve' and into whose likeness we seek to grow should, I believe, allow these 'customer service models' to provoke response.

Scripture and Tradition

The biblical precedent is clear and the early church saw it as a weighty matter incumbent upon all of Jesus' followers, at his own leading:

> I was a stranger and you welcomed me.
> Matthew 25.34–40

For God's people, from Abraham through to you and me, the calling has included welcoming and being hospitable to strangers. Faced with three such visitors by the oaks of Mamre, Abraham does not just pass the time of day over a cuppa; he rolls out the red carpet, readies the fatted calf and Sarah is called on to produce the best from her kitchen (Genesis 8.1–8). Abraham is aiming at excellence; the best is offered to these strangers, though he has no real idea who they are. But what I observe is that any in the church who aim at such high standards in providing welcome today are frequently subjected to derision from those within the church's own ranks. The public, if they do get to hear, are probably staggered to see that the church is setting its sights higher. Paul Scanlon spotlights this clearly: 'The church generally is famous for being a bit of shambles. Jokes are often made about jumble sales and roof funds. No one expects the church to excel at anything it does.'[8]

The passage goes on to say 'Then he took curds and milk and the calf that he had prepared, and set it before them; and he stood by them under the tree while they ate.' He did not just show them a seat either; he watched over them to see they had all they needed. He was attentive and I suspect had they returned he would have been no less effusive in his welcome.

> Welcome does not just stop at the door, it begins here.

And let us not forget that Abraham suggests 'Let a little water be brought, and wash your feet...' reminding us of another such occurrence. Could it be that Jesus, even in the shadow of the cross, needed to leave with us a powerful image of the necessity for us to be welcoming because he knew how soon we would move our eyes, minds and hearts, to other things?

Welcome is also tied very closely with worship. In Isaiah 58 God puts the people of Jerusalem in the picture. If they will share their food with the hungry and welcome poor homeless wanderers, 'salvation will come like the dawn. Yes, your healing will come quickly. Your godliness will lead you forward, and the glory of the LORD will protect you from behind.' (Isaiah 58.7–8) Whilst not wishing to fall into jargon, are not those who as yet do not know the love of Christ for themselves referred to as 'lost' (homeless wanderers), who need to receive the Bread of Life (food for the hungry)? In his commentary on Isaiah, Hawthorne tells us 'the chapter is a *torah* or lesson on proper worship. The criteria for such turns on what God chooses, not what the people like to do. It is more precise: what God requires of any *human being*.'[9] Surely, then, the teaching of doctrines of worship should include 'welcoming the stranger' as a vital component. Keifert's thesis on evangelism and public worship covers this comprehensively, and he observes:

...pastors and parishioners believe that worship and evangelism do not belong together. For these congregational members worship is primarily the care and nurture of the congregational family, a time for bonding and communication, much like time around a family dinner table...other congregations, or sometimes just a few of their members, perceive the challenge of the unannounced visitor as an opportunity.[10]

The New Testament assumes the position of the Old in expecting that welcome will be extended. James recognizes a distortion in the way it can occur in public worship services. It seems that only those whose 'face fits' are being welcomed, that the 'poor person' is being given short shrift and directed to sit out of the way (James 2.1–13). Even that may be a step up from the treatment some people nowadays have received; at least they were being addressed! On a less derisive note though, maybe we are selective in whom we will greet during coffee. The video *Truth on the Streets* tenders a graphic depiction of this.[11] The story is set at a funeral of a man, who in due course is revealed as a transsexual in the process of changing his gender. The pain and rejection evoked by this decision has resulted in his suicide. Each of the mourners recalls their friend, and as Justin, a clothes designer who is gay, tells his tale he includes his own experience of attending church at his deceased Christian friend's encouragement. They had, he enlightens the viewer, taken one *look* at him, read the label and put him back on the shelf— not their type, not good enough, is the implication. The afflictions of the church that James pastored still trouble today.

Welcoming Jesus

As I turn to the final chapters of my Bible, the image of Jesus the Light of the World by Holman Hunt, standing outside the doors of his church waiting to come in, eclipses my minds' eye. In the picture the door has no handle. The doors are not swung wide to welcome him, as one might expect. No, he is stood outside, having to attract attention so that he might receive the welcome of his church (Revelation 3.20). For many today, the church in question at Laodicea depicts what we see in Western Christianity. The church has become lukewarm, apathetic in its prosperity; it has stopped taking its mission seriously and even the Lord has to knock to gain entrance.

While the early church did not rewrite the customs and traditions regarding hospitality, they probably did perceive it in a more comprehensive manner.

> While we may look at hospitable practices of early Christianity and see them as nothing more than good deeds, hospitality was not simply a matter of private virtue. It was embedded in community and a sign of God's presence in that community, and so was an embodiment of a biblical ethic.[12]

And You Welcomed Me by Amy Oden is filled with quotations from early church writers. Augustine directs: 'Acknowledge the duty of hospitality, for by this some have attained unto God.' John Chrysostom exhorts 'the theme of recognizing Christ in the stranger'; from the life of one of the Desert Fathers we read: 'There watchmen are posted to keep an eye out for strangers in need and welcome them as angels.' There is also the less well known St Leoba. She lived in Bischopsheim around 779, helped to Christianize Western Europe and maintained an 'open door' policy. 'She kept open house for all without exception, and even when she was fasting gave banquets and washed the feet of the guests with her own hands, at once the guardian and minister of the practice instituted by our Lord.'[13]

3 The Issue of Introversion— Some Analysis

Why is it, that caring, God-fearing people, like many who have nurtured me in my faith, fall into the trap of being sightless when it comes to the whole issue of welcome?

What makes a church omit cutting its grass for months or leave tatty out of date notices on public boards, thus adding to the image of carelessness? Why is there much talk of needing to grow but no thought about the importance of the first impression—which will often be the only one you get to make?

Moss confirms 'A church will only have once to make a good impression. In fact, if your church fails to make a good impression, they will probably give up church as a lost cause.'[14] Further illustration of this was shared in a conversation lately when I was told that even 20 years afterwards people can still remember every aspect of their first visit to church, especially the details of those who spoke to them!

We really do need to get ourselves out of maintenance mode if we are to begin to put our churches on the map again

Yes, I know that no one wants it to be like this. We are under-staffed, money is short, the majority of our folk are elderly, there are more pressing things on the agenda—but are there? If we do not address some of these evangelistic issues, none of the problems will be solved. We really do need to get ourselves out of maintenance mode, or a stage more fatal, if we are to begin to put our churches on the map again. Even small churches with very limited resources can have an ethos of welcome.

Winding the clock back a little and placing ourselves back in the days before we were members of our churches may help recognize some symptoms. What were the factors that lead us to be 'insiders?' Naturally there will be innumerable answers to that but for those who have ventured into our churches as adults there does appear to be some common ground.

A Family Affair

'Searching' is a word that I have heard often, not just from those whom I have met personally, but also by those whose vocation in life is to ascertain the social and spiritual climate of the day. John Ortberg touches the heart of the matter: 'The yearning to attach and connect, to love and be loved, is the fiercest longing of the soul.'[15]

The opportunities to belong do not exist unless someone comes back on a second and subsequent occasions

'Belonging,' in whatever way that was for us, was almost certainly the key reason we stayed in church, and initial impressions were essential. We need to bear in mind the opportunities to belong do not exist unless someone comes back on a second and subsequent occasions. We all need to belong, to be part of the whole and to be valued in such. But why is that a problem? Well, I consider that the security we receive from belonging can begin to be the trap that allows us to fall into introversion. Further exploration about belonging and believing can be found in *Gone But Not Forgotten*.[16]

Making friends, becoming part of the life of the church and feeling secure, is vital, but if unchecked can lead to being inward-looking. Arriving on a Sunday it is great to see our friends, to know the pages to find and the tunes to songs; we fit, and feel right. When it comes to coffee time, it is great to catch up on news, to share joys and tears, but all too soon our comfort zones only include those like us, in the know, on the inside. We have forgotten the gut-wrenching fear of that first journey over the threshold. We are no longer that stranger. It is wonderful; it is all that we hoped and all the church hoped for us. Days and weeks pass, more insider activities fill our time, we know and are known—a success story for all. The teaching we receive encourages us to reflect on ourselves and our spiritual condition. We are called to prayer and Bible study, which is mostly a solitary activity or something we do with those who are part of the church family. Inevitably as Keifert maintains 'many congregations misunderstand worship as a private family affair.'[17] Family is a fine metaphor for the church—the Bible uses it, for example Galatians 6.10 and Ephesians 3.15—but giving the impression that the church is only for those who already belong is detrimental to the mission Christ set before us (Matthew 28.19–20).

We have forgotten the gut-wrenching fear of that first journey over the threshold

The family is an evocative icon for our modern world where family life has become so chaotic and disparate. Multitudes long for the connectedness its concept, when ordered aright, offers. Church can be a place where familial-like bonds are forged,

13

but birth is its first necessity. New birth is another image used by Paul, but strictly speaking babies are small and expected for 9 months. Newborns in church quite probably come much bigger, fully grown and so the similes, again from Paul, of adoption apply. With language like this, the church has much to offer the 'homeless wanderer,' who is as evident now as in Isaiah's day.

The commendable input we are giving to our members may well be the seed bed of just the problems we are trying to avoid

The very sad thing is that the commendable and necessary input and guidance we are giving to our members may well be the seed bed of just the problems we are trying to avoid.

The Problem of Introspection

Others, though not entirely for the same reason, have considered this problem of introspection. Eaton in framing a theology of encouragement, looks back to the 18th century, when the 'methodist' movement in the English-speaking world began to lay emphasis on experiencing God, resulting in a separation between Calvinists and Armenians. He concludes that the theology developed by both parties resulted in legalism...

> ...but the Calvinist often bore the burden of introspection...Classical high Calvinism has taught a doctrine of 'final perseverance' which, despite its apparently encouraging tendency, actually includes strongly introspective and discouraging elements.[18]

Though his thesis is looking to a different end, his identification of the tendency to introversion is, I believe, correct. Praying, Bible study, church attendance or even witnessing in a mode of self-examination—which is in effect what we teach—engenders introspection. This ethic, whether awareness of it exists or not, has permeated the church's corporate culture and is, in my opinion, characteristic of the problems faced today.

This said, in some sections of the church the pendulum has swung the other way and little if any emphasis is placed on getting serious about your faith. This results in apathetic introspection that seeks only to serve its own needs, forgetting the challenge to offer the Good News to 'all the world.'

John Bowden's thought-provoking book, *Voices in the Wilderness*, challenged churches to look outside their walls at those Jesus would have been meeting and to be more discerning in accepting all that has been handed on to them. Written in 1977, its front cover asks: 'Have churches, like introspective individuals, channelled all their energy towards survival to the point of excluding from their care and concern the very people for whom they exist?' He concludes they have. This infirmity he describes as 'a chronic lingering disease.' Three decades have passed, and the concerns he quite rightly raised are still ignored; our eyes are fixed on the interior of our churches and decline has continued.

Dallas Willard, writing about developing the character of the church, calls the predicament expressed by Bowden 'the vessel trap.' Taking his analogy from Paul's second letter to the Corinthians (2 Corinthians 4.6–7), he too concludes that congregations get so tied up in each other and the internal hows, whys and wherefores that they fail to grow, not just numerically but spiritually as well.[19]

Are there any answers? Well, ever the optimist, I think the prospects are good.

4   Extraversion and Conversion— A Pair of Potentials

The opposite of introversion is extraversion, another word that is not usually associated with church.

Cloistered nuns and quiet medieval clerics bowed in prayer are still very prominently held impressions. Some may recall the celebrated preacher Billy Graham or others of his ilk, but in the main the silent contemplative or erudite ecclesiastic holds sway in the majority of minds.

Borrowing a phrase synonymous with Myers and Briggs,[20] whose theories derived from those of Jung, our churches need to develop their 'shadow side.' I realize this research and resultant training material is concerned with where we draw our emotional resources from and not about how we present ourselves to others—but the terminology lends itself well. Each personality type has an opposite, shadow side, and in order to become a fully rounded person, developing that attribute is essential. The church's profile indicates introspection high on the scale. Assisting it to work in its shadow side will effect transformation and give it a mission imperative.

The problem appears to be that we develop a security in our introversion, but with fear tingeing the edges of our comfort because just maybe things will go awry. New people might shift the balance, things might change—and conceivably for the worse.

Even so, change cannot be avoided, but that is the rub. Taking the risk to make any alterations, to deliver a little equilibrium disturber, to shift a few comfort zones, is a very risky business. Fortunately we have a good model. Jesus knew without a doubt that things could not go on the way they were, that 'church' as he knew it was not fulfilling its God-given function and so he set about his task of unsettling the *status quo*. Thankfully our undertaking is not quite on that scale.

Behaviour Modification

The task is, I propose, similar to 'behaviour modification,' a method I have used in education. This approach, used by behavioural psychologists to adjust conduct, is based on the reinforcement of desired behaviours and ignoring, as far as possible, the undesired. The key is to reinforce the required actions, with praise—which is far more potent than criticism. Identification of the benefits that could be gained from the particular behaviour or pattern of behaviour that you hope to attain further promotes action towards the goal.

Though the task to be undertaken in the church cannot in truth be seen quite in this light, it is similar. It is more a job of helping people to realign their vision, encouraging them to grow and flourish in the confidence they have gained in finding faith and belonging to a community of believers, but without losing sight of where they have come from, so evoking their empathy with the new arrival standing uneasily at the entrance. Identifying the benefits that can be achieved by the changes proposed will strike a chord, people will begin to see new possibilities and vision will grow. When people care enough about an issue they do something about it.

When people care enough about an issue they do something about it

In short, we need to stimulate concern for the stranger, so that the culture of the church becomes such that everyone's agenda includes it, reducing responsibility on the few. This will require teaching, including prompting a recall of the feelings aroused from people new to church, thus enabling our congregations to offer a welcome worthy of the one on whose behalf that hospitality is actually offered. Even minor gains should be celebrated, in a public forum preferably, thus boosting morale, breeding confidence and building faith for additional endeavours. The testimony of someone who has felt welcomed is one example and this could be in the church magazine or similar. It need not necessarily be a spoken testimony—which some would find too challenging.

n short, we need to stimulate concern for the stranger

But this change is not as simple to achieve as its sounds. Expecting an immediate reframing of ways of thinking and behaving in people who have lived in a particular way for many years is unrealistic. Certain ways of doing things becomes so engrained that people find it impossible to envisage different ways of being, and so it is wholly unreasonable to imagine that people who have been exposed to one sermon on being welcoming will 'get it' and embrace the new direction, even at an intellectual level, let alone behaviourally.

Porter, writing about using behaviour orientation, identifies that changing strategic behaviour begins with the leadership.[21] He draws out seven points to consider—I have adapted some of the language though not the emphasis.

Consistency

Align the beliefs and values of the leadership team. All need to be enthused by similar values. Consistency must be seen between what is said and what is done, evidenced in the messages delivered whatever the form, and stated consistently for at least twelve months to embed the message.

Learning

This begins with those in leadership before it can be successfully transmitted to others. Workshops are most effective where groups of leaders and members work together to tackle the implementation of new values but within an agenda and structure that ensures the new values and ways of working are established simultaneously. This learning is collaborative and has the capability to establish powerful support networks across the entire membership.

Courage

Second only to learning, the hallmark of great leaders is courage. Be bold without being reckless. Be assured in your approach but in a style that encourages others to step out in a like manner, which may mean working in your own shadow side.

Communication

The best way to achieve some sense of unity of purpose is by the very best communication. Empowered organizations are those where everyone is as clear as the leadership about the priorities. Every single member should be personally responsible for making communication a real priority. In everything, whether it is in a personal encounter, a large group event, a Sunday service, or meetings with those outside church structures, communication is always happening. There will be an audience, whether planned or not, hence the need for consistency. This means constantly championing the cause, talking about progress and living the values.

Engagement

Engagement is a process of enrolling people in the pursuit of a challenge. It may involve convincing them to give up or forego something in exchange for an unknown future benefit. The role of leaders in engagement is to make the challenge known, to spell out the hopes, to build the organization's self-confidence and to use their powers of persuasion to bring over doubters. Engagement is about getting people to behave in a particular way because they want to, not because they are told to!

Mobilization

Communication is a foundation stone of engagement but you need to go further and think in terms of mobilization. This means moving people from a position of ignorance to becoming active and supportive players. It involves them in a personal journey, from awareness that something is going on, but not really appreciating how they will be affected, through understanding, on to commitment to the change and the desire to be part of it. From there it involves moving to participation in action and finally recognition of the results.

Appraisal

Regular checks on progress are essential.

Porter concludes:

So, when your company decides to embark on a new strategic direction be prepared to invest as much if not more effort in aligning behaviour to strategy and take some months to do it. Do not wait to find out that the message is not getting through; make it a priority to plan and implement some real support to help people get the message so that they can start to behave strategically.[22]

In essence what we are talking about is the naissance of building community, but community that is approachable, accessible and hospitable. What is needed is community that presents itself as cared for and so caring of others, a place where God's love is shared not just with the established people but with the uninitiated as well.

5

Preparing the Way—
Some Best Practice Shared

How to undertake this mission will depend to some extent on the situation in which you find yourself and the resources at your disposal.

All the ideas listed later are adaptable and manageable even in a small church. The starting point is appropriate evangelism through the worship. Keifert hits the nail on the head:

> Sunday morning worship has become a moment of evangelism whether Christians like it or not—indeed, whether they are prepared or not. The critical question is thus not whether we will choose to do evangelism but whether the challenge of evangelism that is thrust upon us is being effectively met.[23]

Weekday services, occasional offices, visits from school, tourism, and so on all provide similar moments of contact when first impressions need to be on the agenda. Each of these areas are worthy of further consideration in any church in order to demonstrate an ethos of welcome.

Hospitality Audit

Review is a good way to begin. The situation in your church might be much better that you think. Get everyone to complete the audit set out in the Appendix. This will help put the issue on everyone's agenda, show up false perceptions and provide a tool for discussion. Perhaps you could also ask an third party to cast a fresh eye over the scenario using the audit form as a guide. Another idea to get the reflection process stirred is to be a visitor yourself at another church, consider how it feels and observe what they do.

Look Right

This is not a section of the Green Cross Code, but a reminder that physical appearances are important. In many cases we cannot change our buildings but we can make the very best of them. Clean, tidy, warm, light enough—and so the list could go on. Get several groups of people, children, young people (especially if they do not go to church!), young families, people out of work, professionals, some folk with disabilities and older people to walk around and report on how the church facilities could be more welcoming.

Act Right

Preparation for a service is often a flurry of activity that can give adverse signals. Ensure those who will welcome are ready in time and have all they need to do the job. One task I see happening often is service/notice sheets being propelled into hymn books as folk arrive, thus focusing attention away and preventing a warm greeting. Some churches have both sidespersons and 'greeters' which can work well. However, being too effusive can be overwhelming for the first-timer, who is most probably uneasy already.

Consider the directions which are given during the service. Some of the most upset people I have dealt with in this area are those who felt excluded from the worship because lack of 'stage directions' meant they could not join in. And though this is not the place for a weighty discussion on the pros and cons of an open communion table, please contemplate the words of invitation used. I am grieved more than words can say to hear that only 'insiders' are welcome to meet with the Lord at his table. We can bless people even if our theology will not allow us to have them partake. Jesus, I am sure, never envisaged a holy clique!

Provide Right

People do want to be welcomed. But careful handling is needed, particularly because (as was highlighted earlier) church is an unknown quantity for most people, leaving them feeling disconcerted. Pew cards, welcome booklets/ packs/videos/DVDs are valuable items to have on offer and will aid people's confidence for a return visit. Perhaps offer a recorded service so they can become familiar with what happens.

Devise ways to ensure that new folk are noticed. In a big church even have registers, completed by nominated persons discretely, who can ensure that pastoring happens effectively because missing people, especially the vulnerable, can be identified easily and new folk are noticed on their first visit. Be prepared in advance for follow up, for their return and for their integration into church life, certainly look out for them next time they come. Some churches offer regular Sunday lunches, in homes of members, to cultivate friendships. My home church held regular 'newcomers tea parties' where, as a good afternoon tea was being consumed, the team introduced themselves (remember this need not just be clergy or paid staff), as well as offering brief details of local and wider church matters appropriate to the stage of the journey. Run a regular initial nurture course such as *Alpha* or *Emmaus* (regular could mean annually) so that folk have something to look ahead to.

Having contacted some 100 churches to discover their methods more ideas came to light:

- welcome boards displaying relevant information for new folk
- board of photos and names of key church folk
- ensuring church contact details are on all literature
- church history—book/boards[24]
- prayer request boards
- visitors'/ first-timers' book
- happy bags of quiet toys and games for children
- bookstall/library
- Christian Enquiry Agency produce high quality 'Contact Cards' which can be used in pews, on welcome desks, in welcome packs, and so on.[25]
- social events of various types are points of welcome
- street warden scheme
- packs to welcome new folk to the area including other helpful local information such as doctors, dentists and nurseries
- vicar's surgery hours (not so threatening for those with questions)

Preparing ourselves to welcome new people is not the easiest task in the world. It needs constant vigilance but it will pay its dividends both as new people are enabled to find faith and encompassed into the body of Christ and that entire body grows in love and service of, and for, the One who first loved us.

I leave the final word with Jean Vanier, founder of L'Arche, communities of life with those who have developmental disabilities.

A Christian community constantly calls its members to share, welcome, become poorer and go beyond their resources to a truer love.[26]

Bibliography 6

John Bowden, *Voices in the Wilderness* (London: SCM Press, 1977)

Steve Chalke with Sue Radford, *New Era/New Church* (London: Harper Collins, 1999)

Leslie J Francis and Philip Richter, *Gone but not forgotten—Church leaving and returning* (London, DLT, 1998)

Vivian A Hall, *Be My Guest* (Chicago: Moody Press, 1979)

Gerald F Hawthorne, *Word Biblical Commentary, Volume 25: Isaiah 34–66* (Dallas: Word Books, 1987)

Patrick R Keifert, *Welcoming the Stranger—a public theology of worship and evangelism* (Minneapolis: Ausburg Fortress, 1992)

Paul R Nixon, *Fling Open the Doors—giving the church away to the community* (Nashville: Abingdon Press, 2002)

Amy G Oden (editor), *And you welcomed me—a sourcebook on hospitality in the early church* (Nashville: Abingdon Press, 2001)

John Ortberg, *Everybody's Normal Till You Get To Know Them* (Grand Rapids: Zondervan, 2003)

Paul Scanlon, *God's Fingerprint—Principles for fruitful lives and churches* (London: Hodder & Stoughton, 1999)

Dallas Willard, *Renovation of the Heart—Putting on the Character of Christ* (London: Inter Varsity Press, 2002)

Appendix A—Hospitality Audit

Is your church easy to find? Do you need new signs on major roads near your church? Are you in yellow pages, etc? _____

Is your church's name easy to read from the road?	YES	NO
Can entrances be identified easily?	YES	NO
Is the general appearance, interior and exterior, including any gardens, of your church well maintained and attractive?	YES	NO
Are there a few parking spots close to the building which are reserved for the disabled or visitors?	YES	NO
Are pathways, the entrance, and the interior spaces of the church easy to navigate for persons in wheelchairs or with other mobility concerns?	YES	NO

If you have toilets how do they look? Are they clean, tidy and suitably stocked? What access is there for people with disabilities?

Are all rooms in the church clearly marked? Again, has access for people with disabilities been facilitated?	YES	NO
Are the notice boards, inside and out, current? New people are more likely than regular members to read them.	YES	NO
Are there stacks of out-of-date notice sheets, old magazines, and so on which should be discarded?	YES	NO
Is current, attractive, up-to-date information about your church available to offer to new people?	YES	NO
Is there sufficient lighting?	YES	NO

What provision is made for children? _____

Are the instructions to enable people to join the worship   YES NO
made clear? Remember many people have never been to
any church before.

Are large print copies of prayer books, hymn books, Bibles and handouts
available? Is hearing amplification and a loop system available? Has consideration been made for other disabled folk and their needs?

_____

Do the notices and other 'insider' references make guests feel excluded? Do
people identify themselves?

_____

_____

Do you have greeters positioned at the entrances to the   YES NO
church? Are greeters and sidespeople prepared to welcome
guests? Do you offer training for those who undertake this
task?

Are all members of the congregation prepared to welcome   YES NO
guests? Would training for this be helpful?

Do you provide refreshments? How are they advertised? Would a newcomer
know where to go? _____

_____

Are members aware of new folk, willing to chat to and   YES NO
introduce them to others?

Do you have a system whereby information about new   YES NO
folk can be obtained and so make follow up possible?

Have you interviewed people who have recently visited   YES NO
your church and asked them for feedback on their experience? Have you talked both to people who have continued
to come and to some who only came once?

What other areas should you consider? For example, what does the telephone
greeting or answer phone message convey? What about the offering? Is it
better to leave a plate in the entrance hall near sidespersons or to pass it
around during the service? _____

_____

Finally, do you practise the McCulloch 3 minute rule: chat   YES NO
with visitors before friends after the service?

Appendix B—An Exercise: In Their Shoes?

One of the issues we face as we become integrated into our churches is we soon forget how it feels to be the newcomer.

This session is designed to help to consider those who are new to our churches, the problems they have to face in order to be able to join in and feel able to return again.

On the Outside

Get into groups of four or more. All but one of you link arms to form a circle. The one who is not included now has to find a way to get into the group, to join. Take it in turns to be the separated person then sit and discuss. For some it may have been easy to ask for admittance, for others not. *How did it feel*? Discuss other times when you have been new or when you have been excluded from a group—first visit to an established group of some sort, finding a seat in meeting or canteen, asking for directions in a new place especially if there is a language barrier.

What Do We Call Them?

I have called this exercise 'In *their* shoes?' How appropriate do you think that is? What do you call the new folk at your church? Guest, Newcomer, Stranger, Visitor, Outsider or First-Timer? Are these terms appropriate and how does these different terms affect how we deal with the people? What might we call them and how could this affect our approach?

Decreasing Discomfort

'Familiarity breeds contempt' the old saying goes. But the unknown, for us all, is unnerving. Regular attendance means we forget how ill at ease folk might feel on that first visit especially if that visit is an important occasion like a wedding or baptism or emotionally charged like a funeral. How might we make things easier? In groups of four or more devise an exercise to use with church members that could enable them to empathize. For example, teachers are made to write with their non-dominant hand when trying to understand how it feels to learn to write. Each group can then put to their activity to the test on everyone present. Discuss together how it *felt*.

Communication

Communication is a two-way process. It includes sending and receiving messages. Like transmitters we send out and pick up signals continually and in many ways. Communication starts with an idea in the sender's mind which is converted to words or signs and becomes a message which is then conveyed to a recipient. When the receiver's idea matches that of the sender effective communication has taken place.

There are two main types of communication, the verbal and the non-verbal. In your group try to think of examples of both. Consider these not only in the light of Sunday morning but for the entire culture of your church. What message, for example, does the church garden give? How might your tone of voice alter when addressing a family member and someone you know? They say a smile can say a thousand words, what else do we say silently as people and as a community? Remember that although we usually associate listening with our ears we receive as much information from someone's non-verbal signs as we do the spoken ones.

Try this role play exercise. Take turns to communicate to your group the following without words:

Happiness/Sadness/Anger/Fear/Uncertainty/Fun/Excitement/
Hunger/Disappointment/Delight/Aloneness

How easy was this? Did the 'receivers' get them all correct?

Appendix C—Bible Study

A helpful Bible study from Luke's gospel by Alan Bartlett can be found on the supporting web page at www.grovebooks.co.uk under Online Resources. The page includes the text of the study and a link which enables the study to be downloaded as a document.

Notes

1   www.christian-research.org.uk
2   Steve Chalke with Sue Radford, *New Era / New Church* (Harper Collins, 1999).
3   Vivian A Hall, *Be My Guest* (Chicago: Moody Press, 1979) p 155
4   www.faithwalkonline.org/welcoming.htm
5   www.newLifeMinistries-NLM.org
6   Philip Richter and Leslie J Francis, *Gone But Not Forgotten—Church Leaving and Returning* (DLT, 1998).
7   Paul Nixon, *Fling open the Doors—giving the church away to the community* (Nashville: Abingdon Press) p 82.
8   Paul Scanlon, *God's Fingerprint—Principles for fruitful lives and churches* (London: Hodder & Stouton, 1999) p 110.
9   Gerald F Hawthorne, *Word Biblical Commentary, Volume 25: Isaiah 34–66* (electronic ed).
10 Patrick R Keifert, *Welcoming the Stranger—a public theology of worship and evangelism* (Minneapolis: Ausburg Fortres, 1992) p 4.
11 www.eauk.org
12 Amy G Oden, *And you welcomed me*, p 16.
13 *ibid*, p 74.
14 www.NewLifeMinistries-NLM.org
15 John Ortberg, *Everybody's Normal Till You Get To Know Them*, p 18.
16 Philip Richter and Leslie J Francis, *Gone But Not Forgotten*.
17 P R Keifert , *Welcoming the Stranger,* cover notes.
18 Michael Eaton, *A Theology of Encouragement*, p 15.
19 Dallas Willard, *Renovation of the Heart – Putting on the Character of Christ* (London: Inter Varsity Press, 2002) p 27.
20 Myers-Briggs Personality Indicator Test. MBTI is a trademark registered to Consulting Psychologists Inc.
21 www.brackenbury.co.uk/word-on-the-street/translating_strategy_into_behavi.htm
22 *ibid.*
23 P R Keifert, *Welcoming the Stranger*, p 3.
24 Richard Askew, Grove Evangelism booklet Ev 38 *From Strangers to Pilgrims: Evangelism and the Church Tourist* is helpful here.
25 www.christianity.org.uk/materials_resources
26 Jean Vanier, *Community and Growth* (DLT), quoted in Peter Price, *The Church as the Kingdom—A New Way of Being the Church* (Basingstoke: Marshall Pickering, 1987).